Advance Praise for
THE CROOKED CHRISTMAS TREE

"Damian Chandler masterfully captivates the reader with a simple account, revealing a timeless message of redemption and hope. Make no mistake, the heart of this book brings the reader to a place of encouragement and complete transformation."

—Parnell M. Lovelace, Jr., Lovelace Leadership Connection

"This story is heartwarming and life changing. Damian writes with such beauty and profundity that the story of Christ and His love should never be the same for anyone who reads this insightful book. THE CROOKED CHRISTMAS TREE should be a new song for all to sing."

—C. Wesley Knight, Professor of Religion and Preaching, Oakwood University

"From shame to shopping, tinsel to the Trinity, Damian Chandler weaves together the deep truths of theology and the trappings of every family's Christmas, and he does it with prose that shines like a Christmas star. Read this book, and you'll never look at your Christmas tree the same."

—Ryan Sanders, author of *Unbelievable: Examining the Unlikely Beauty of the Christian Story*

"Don't wait for Easter or Christmas, this is a book for any season in life. Damian in his unique delightful unraveling, draws your whole family into a story with multiple layers, turning the complex into simple and bringing value to your life. In a time when we are fragmented, this is one book that can help build stronger communities, stronger families, stronger people in Jesus."

—Japhet J. De Oliveira, Co-Founder,
One project

"I found myself in love with a crooked tree, less aware of my imperfections, and completely overwhelmed by the goodness of God, all from the pages of a book. THE CROOKED CHRISTMAS TREE brilliantly brings to light an unconditional love we all long for."

—Stephen Chandler, Senior Pastor,
Destiny Harvest Church

"Deeply spiritual, exquisitely written, this book will shine the light of God's love into the hearts of all who read it."

—Wintley Phipps, vocal artist, CEO and
Founder, U.S. Dream Academy

"Damian Chandler gives you artistry and therapy all in the same breath. As so many are languishing in guilt and shame, his narrative helps us cast off self-inflicted anxiety while we grab hold of Jesus' amazing grace."

—Chaplain Michael Polite, Campus Ministries, Andrews University

"THE CROOKED CHRISTMAS TREE is sure to be a timeless classic. The way Damian compares the crooked Christmas tree with the brokenness and crookedness of everyday people is brilliant. This book will speak to the heart and soul of every person who reads it. If you've ever felt you aren't good enough, attractive enough, or smart enough, this book is for you. Not only is THE CROOKED CHRISTMAS TREE perfect for the holidays, the content is relevant year round."

—Jeremy Anderson, author, Founder, Grace Tour

"More than a book, it offers slices of real life with a real God who loves real people in a real world. Damian Chandler is a fresh and fascinating voice."

—Jesse Wilson, Director, Bradford-Cleveland-Brooks Leadership Center, Oakwood University

"From the first page, Damian Chandler pulls the reader into this charming, witty, and colorful tale about a crooked tree, our imperfect lives, and the extravagant grace of God. Read this book—you'll find yourself immersed in the story and in love with the Gospel."

—Tyler Stewart, Young Adult Pastor,
Loma Linda University Church

"I loved reading THE CROOKED CHRISTMAS TREE. Most of all, I loved the clarity of the Gospel presented in this heartfelt story. In my mind, the book was similar to some New Testament parables in that I can see myself in multiple roles. I am the Crooked Tree. I am the adult, thinking I have to decorate the 'crookedness' of my life. I am the innocent child who recognizes the beauty of the crooked tree and loves it as it is. This will be one of the books I pull out and read year after year."

—Keith Jeffries, Owner, Huntsville Havoc
professional hockey team

"THE CROOKED CHRISTMAS TREE is a powerful and passionate reminder of God's unconditional love for us. It will leave you both challenged and overwhelmed by a God who so recklessly pursues, embraces, and cherishes us. Damian Chandler reminds us of God's unashamed love for humanity in spite of all our various quirks and foibles."

—Pastor Seth Yelorda, Lead Pastor, Westminster Good Samaritan Church

The Crooked Christmas Tree

The Beautiful Meaning of Jesus' Birth

Damian Chandler

New York   Nashville

FaithWords
Hachette Book Group
1290 Avenue of the Americas, New York, NY 10104
faithwords.com
twitter.com/faithwords

First Edition: October 2017

FaithWords is a division of Hachette Book Group, Inc. The FaithWords
name and logo are trademarks of Hachette Book Group, Inc.

The publisher is not responsible for websites (or their content) that are
not owned by the publisher.

The Hachette Speakers Bureau provides a wide range of authors for
speaking events. To find out more, go to www.hachettespeakersbureau.com
or call (866) 376-6591.

Scripture quotations are from The Holy Bible, New International
Version® NIV®. Copyright © 1973, 1978, 1984, 2011 by Biblica, Inc.®
Used by permission of Biblica, Inc.® All rights reserved worldwide.

Library of Congress Cataloging-in-Publication Data has been applied for.

ISBNs: 978-1-4789-1837-0 (hardcover), 978-1-5460-3323-3 (ebook)

Printed in the United States of America

LSC-C

10 9 8 7 6 5 4 3 2 1

To my tribe, Tanzy, Zoe, Salem and Levi.
Your love is life to me.

CONTENTS

Contents

The Crooked
Christmas Tree

THE ONE

The Christmas tree hunt was on! The hunt for The One.

We were herded into the store, drawn by flashing lights and Silent Nights, and we were not alone. Every road seemed to empty into this parking lot, as many a GPS declared, "You have reached your final destination." SUVs pulled between yellow stripes, turning off the engine and lights.

Neighbor became the competition for pined treasure. We gave each other suspicious looks masked by pleasant hellos. No one wants to pick through anyone else's tree leftovers, so we drew a line in the sand. We went left. The other family went right.

Wayward glimpses over the shelves, down

the aisles, and around the corners were all we had to inform us of their strategy. Maybe it was no different than ours. But we all knew there would be a victor, and it would be the family that found The One.

THE CROOKED
TREE

This live Christmas tree thing started because every good television family had this tradition, and long before I was married, I had decided that I wanted Christmas traditions. Once I found me a wife and we had some children, the next thing on the list was traditions.

So my wife and I decided that a live Christmas tree would be the first of our many family traditions. My wife, the timely one, wanted to have the tree up the day after Thanksgiving, and I wanted the smell of fresh pine in the house. So the tradition became that we took the kids to a lot the day after Thanksgiving, they chose a real tree, and I put it up.

My wife chooses the price point, and my

job is to guide the kids to a few good trees, because crooked trees really bother me. Not as easy as it would seem, because for what we are willing to spend, there often seems to be more duds than studs. But this year there were crowds of seven-foot green beauties. They wore their branches like models in Paris, boasting their willingness to belittle themselves, to be tied on to the roof of my car and to take residence in our modest home.

My daughter walked past these boasting beauties, unimpressed. At the end of the line, behind the prima donnas, stood a reject. To say it stood was to be kind. I almost had to tilt my head sideways to look at it. It seemed to know its shortcomings because it hid, cowered behind all the "worthy" choices, almost hoping not to be seen. For if it was never seen, it could never be rejected.

Before I could speak, my daughter had already walked past lines of lovely trees and was standing in front of the castaway. Think she might have even looked at it sideways as it shamefully looked back.

"This one. I want this one. What do you think, Salem?"

"Yep, that is the one."

Oh the horror. I immediately moved to damage control, trying to convince my daughter of the worthiness of the other suitors. How could I spend my entire Christmas looking at a crooked tree? "Are you sure?" I asked her.

"Yes, Daddy."

"What about that one?"

But she shook her head. She was already in love. Already attached.

Before it had proven its worth or shown its creed, my kids were already attached to that crooked Christmas tree. Before they checked its record or its life trajectory, they were already in love. That is who they are. The new toy with the vaulted pedigree and high price will never replace that old and broken relic. That brand-new blanket with their names embroidered and initials embossed will sit unwrapped, new smell intact, while the one with stitched-up holes and dark patches, with mold, is the one sought on nights when they are cold. For they are in love. They are attached.

But this must be different. To grow attached while a blanket molds in hand is one thing, but to buy a moldy blanket is clearly another. Why purchase something knowing its defects and shortcomings? Why look for the least beautiful? The least admirable? The least attractive?

I presented my final arguments like a savvy lawyer before the court. This tree was guilty of the high treason of crookedness and deserved a life sentence on the shelf without the possibility of purchase.

But the jury would not be convinced.

Plus my wife was giving me that stare. It was supposed to be the kids' choice.

But wasn't I supposed to guide them around choices detrimental to their health—and mine?

She's still staring.

Fine! We'll pay for this crooked tree and take this crooked tree home. And this crooked tree will ruin Christmas.

WHY THIS TREE?

I could not force my face to smile, or will my heart to be happy. Yes, I had conceded. Standing in line, card drawn, now swiped—it was final. The tree was theirs...mine. But my concession did nothing to squelch my mind's screaming question. I tried to be okay with it. But every time I even glanced in its direction, that question "Why this tree?" boiled over like milk on the stove. Only this realization stopped me from throwing myself on the floor in that store, banging my head on the linoleum while screaming, "Why this tree?"

I remembered lying on my back on a dark, cloudless night and looking out into the vastness of space. Everything that my eyes could see was only the universe's first page. Its final chapter—15.5 billion light-years from Earth—was *beyond* far away. Within that known expanse were billions of galaxies, many infinitely more impressive than our Milky Way. Within the Milky Way were billions of stars painted against the black of outer space, many of them infinitely more brilliant than our sun. And even among the planets of our solar system, our planet pales in comparison to massive gas giants like Jupiter. Compared to Earth, Jupiter is massive. Compared to Jupiter, the sun is a monster. Compared to Arcturus, one of the closest stars, our sun is a dot. I lay there lost in the fact that the Earth was essentially invisible.

Why would God choose to expend His greatest collateral on something so insignificant? You would think there were beings more worthy than us. What about the angels? Why not save them? After all, they had spent eternity doing God's bidding—bowing, holying, flying, declaring. Yet when one-third of them fell over the same stick that tripped us earthlings up, there was no emptying of heaven's coffers to redeem them.* But for fools with a willful addiction to eating what was clearly forbidden,† God chose to risk everything, the only beloved one.‡

Instead of struggling, I found it was enough to say to myself that in some ways God is like my kids. Woefully attracted to crooked trees.

---

* See Revelation 12:3–9.
† See Genesis 3:6.
‡ See John 3:16.

THAT OTHER
FAMILY

Standing at the cash register, I saw them again—that *other* family. They had spent a longer time in the forest of choices. But now they emerged from around the corner, tree hoisted overhead, a champion. They placed it on the ground and huddled around their selection like a team calling some secret play.

And what a play it was. They had found The One. The green of its needles. The grace of its branches. It was flawless. The dad turned it by its trunk, and it spun like a ballerina on pointed toes. He flashed a pitied look in our direction with an obligatory and condescending smile. Then they took a slow walk to the cashier, a royal parade, and every tree bowed in obeisance. Including ours.

They had their selection...and unfortunately we had ours. The antithesis of beauty. The enemy of grace. I approached the cashier, chin to chest, lowered by the weight of his contemptuous grin. He would pay his money for pined perfection, and I would pay mine for its cross-eyed twin sister.

FULLY AWARE

Isn't it amazing what we are willing to pay for? Have you been to one of those Build-A-Bear stores? My daughter dragged me in one day like a dog to a bath, and what I saw was shocking. Every accessory a bear doesn't need. Shirts and shoes and bags and an astronaut suit. Basketballs and footballs and a cheerleading uniform. And the prices! When an outfit for a stuffed bear costs more than the clothes I am wearing, there is a problem.

But at some point someone was willing to pay for those stuffed bears and their outrageous outfits. Were they any different from the bears at the dollar store? No. But we were willing to pay more for them. And like my tree, their value is whatever we are willing to pay.

No one had pulled the wool over my eyes. They had not hidden the price. Or posted an exaggerated picture on eBay to con or connive. I knew exactly what the tree looked like. I had seen its attributes, and I was aware of its defects. I looked at the price tag, I walked up to the cashier, and I paid for it. In doing so, I declared to the world that to me the tree was worth the price I'd paid.

God, being fully informed of who we were, walked up to the cashier and paid the highest price for our salvation. Our sin, our defaults, did not catch Him by surprise. We did not pull the stuffing over His eyes. Yet He was not willing to walk away, to leave us to reap death's bitter harvest, to shred humankind in sin's mulch machine.* He made His investment, fully aware of the product.

And what an investment to make. Its value is in the word *only*: "rare, unique."† There were

---

* See Romans 6:23.
† See John 3:16.

no other begotten sons. Jesus was the only one He had. God went back to heaven's vault and pulled out the family treasure. Then He spent it, exchanging it for broken merchandise.

There are many who wonder whether God has given up on us, whether He has us marked for the compost heap. We are valuable to God. So valuable that He was willing to purchase our salvation. He is fully invested in us, and His investment declares our value. So if you, like me, have ever struggled with self-worth or self-esteem, the answer to your worth is not locked in someone else's approval. Your value is determined by what God, being fully informed, was willing to pay for you.

I PAID FOR THIS

We got home. And as usual everyone piled out of the car, leaving me to be the pack mule. While the kids ran and the wife relaxed, I was left to figure out how to get this tree off the roof of my car and into the house, and that, my friends, was no easy feat. The guys at the store make putting these monsters on your car look easy. But pulling into the driveway, I realized that they don't follow you home to take them off.

Eventually, one volunteer showed up. My four-year-old son. Already well on the way to earning his man card, he looked for every opportunity to prove he deserved one. But since he's only three feet and change, his eagerness is often unmatched by his muscle. His heart was in it, but his hands could barely hold it. Despite his valiant efforts, this challenge was simply beyond his reach. So I would have to face the beast alone.

Cut some cords. Get a good grip. Hoist above head. Make sure there is just enough strain on the face for my wife to think her man is strong. Then I threw the tree to the garage floor, staring it down, hands on my hips, disgusted. Still couldn't believe it. How had I allowed this travesty? Why was I so helpless to save my brood from such outright depravity? With no salvation in sight, the only thing left to do was to put the crooked tree up. We needed a tree, and I was definitely not going out to buy another one.

I went to free the tree stand from its eleven-month banishment. It's funny how little I care about that thing for most of the year, and then in December it becomes the MVP. Turned the tree over. What? There's no hole. Every tree knows that there are only two types of Christmas tree stands in the world. The one with four screws, sold in stores with free coffee and chocolate s'mores. And the brutish one with the spike in the middle, evidence that it was forged by the descendant son of a Viking.

This is common tree knowledge. And this tree should have known by the lowliness of my vehicle and the multiplicity of offspring that there was no way I could have afforded the former. So to show up at my house without a hole was unconscionable.

I was officially mad. I was mad that the kids who chose the tree were now playing tag. I was mad that the wife who affirmed their horrid choice was on the phone with a girlfriend. I was mad because I was forced to buy a crooked tree and I was going to have to work to put it up. Trust me. The only thing that stood between that tree and a mulch machine was the fact that I paid for it, and I was not about to shred my $39.99.

I was mad at it, but I had just paid for it. And the fact that I'd paid for it made its value greater than its troubles. Anger was reduced to frustration. Frustration was subdued by reality. I called a cease-fire, and I signed the peace treaty, even though I had not yet seen the tree through God-like eyes.

MY NAME IS ON
YOUR TITLE

This tree was stubborn. But so was I. I drilled my second hole because after drilling the first, the thing looked more crooked than it had at the store.

I was finally finished. "Let's get this escapade over with," I told the tree, because by this time I just didn't care. "Whatever the angle of your lean, I am officially done. Stand up!"

It tried.

"Be straight."

It leaned.

"Get right."

Like a senior with osteoporosis, its spine just would not cooperate. It could not will itself to rightness, unmake its crooked trunk. Mine were not the first eyes to squint while looking at it, the first face to express chagrin. My daughter's head had not been the first to tilt sideways while staring at it. Somewhere in its heartwood it knew that the horizon was not hung on an angle. But for all of its efforts and daily declarations, it could not make right what had been so horribly wrong. And so it gave in to its lean.

Crookedness was its condition, no fault of its own. It had not chosen its own seed. Or planted that seed in soil far from life-giving light. Or starved the seed of needful water. That was just its lot. But its condition became its label and destiny.

I have a crooked trunk. Condition.

I am a crooked tree. Label.

And that is all I will ever be. Destiny.

It leaned. I threw my hands up in surrender. I would no longer strive with something that had seemingly given up on itself.

I dragged that thing through my garage
door, branches holding on to the doorpost as
if to protest my decision to even bring it inside.

"Two Christmas bulbs and some multicolored lights and I've done my job."

I was about to walk away angry and tired,
but couldn't. I was unable to leave the tree like
that. It was in my house. And in my house, the
condition of my tree was a reflection on me. No
matter the tree's history, as long as it was in my
house, it was my issue. No one was going to
stand in front of my tree and tilt their head sideways to look at it. My visitors were not going to
ask what the tree's problem was. The tree had an
owner, and its condition was my responsibility.

David, the Psalmist, boasted, "The earth is
the LORD's and everything in it."* Don't know

---

* Psalm 24:1

how much of a boast that is. Have you taken a peek at our earth lately? It's a mess. Yet despite that, God's name is still on the title.

David is not simply declaring God's royal reign over this earth. David is declaring that the earth and everything in it is still God's responsibility. Good and bad belong to Him. Its victories and even its failures. And He has no plans of distancing His name from it. Even as we destroy His masterpiece, God still commands that we celebrate His ownership and creative patent every week. Long forgotten, buried under more "important" topics, is God's call for us to celebrate the fact that He is still the titleholder.

He still celebrates the fact that we belong to Him. He celebrates me and reminds me, "My name is still on your title. You are my responsibility. My crooked tree."

EXPOSED

There it stood. Naked... feeling the full weight of its shame. Crowds of trees long gone, there was no one left to hide behind. Not yet dressed in Christmas fancies that would cover the multitude of blemishes. No interesting background distracting my attention. It screamed at me, "Dress me. Put something on me. A bulb, a light, a star. Something. Don't just stand there and look at me. Please don't look at me. Dress me. I feel...exposed."

Limbs drooped in submission, it had reached the point of giving up. How could something so sad, so deformed, ever be a symbol of happiness and celebration?

"Could I ever really be the home of gifts, the mecca to which curious children would make their pilgrimage to guess and wonder? The focal point around which someone might dance and sing? Me?"

Branches rounded like shoulders, it seemed to want to disappear into the shadows of some darkened, forgotten corner. It would have run, if it had feet. Slept its life away, if it had some sheets. But in the absence of bed or feet, the shadows of our living room beckoned as the best cover for its shame.

Shame thrives under cover and grows until it completely consumes and destroys. And shadows are a slave master that uses the chains of secrecy and silence to hold us bound.* The only way to be free of its slavery is full, uncomfortable exposure to the light.

I realized that the crooked tree had spent most of its existence in the shadows of other trees with stronger branches, bigger trunks, greater symmetry. And those others absorbed the light that should have been its own.

---

* See Brené Brown's 3 Steps to Break The Cycle of Shame video.

"Maybe if I had full exposure to sunlight, my limbs would not have been so crooked."

Shame gave birth to regret, and regret to self-pity. Self-pity did its poisonous work, inviting the crooked tree to wallow in things it couldn't change and ignore the things it could. But the longer the crooked tree remained in the shadows, the more it dismissed pity as life-killing, and the space it vacated was quickly filled with anger. Then an inner defiance.

And so it stood in my living room, not yet retreating to the comfort of shadows. It stood not knowing if I would accept it. But it dared to face rejection. It stood. It stood in the light, in all its crookedness, willing to allow me to inspect it, even in its shame. It took courage to stand exposed.

It stood, and I stood with it. No longer was it just the tree that my kids had picked. The one I was willing to pay for on the budget set by my wife. It was now my tree! And as long as it was willing to stand, I would stand with it.

ON THE STEPS OF
A STRIP CLUB

That had not been the first time I stood with someone who had that kind of courage. In fact, while in a town to preach, I met courage sitting on the steps of a strip club.

I had seen it on the way to the church... the strip club. Who could miss it? *Is that building in the shape of a woman's breasts?* Like a golden monument to debauchery, it stood boldly on its corner, daring anyone to object. All the other cars whizzed by as if driving by a Starbucks on a sunny day. I tried not to look. Twisted my head the other way. But finally, I turned to the pastor who was driving me and asked, "What's the story on the heavily breasted building?"

"Since the 1970s, the Booby Trap building has changed hands a few times. There have been meetings and protests and letters and arguments. No change," he replied.

The building stood defiant.

Ills we feel helpless to cure, we choose to ignore. Inconvenient reality. But every time we drove by, I could look in no other direction. Then, on my last day, before my last sermon, in the shadow of that shameful building, I saw two women sitting on the steps of the club, seemingly waiting to clock in.

I thought of the top three places a pastor should never be caught dead in: a bar, unless he was offering communion; a jail, unless he was doing prison ministry; and, well, a strip club for any reason. No ministry applications for that location.

"Pull over," I asked the pastor driving the car.

The bewildered look on his face as he let his guest pastor out in the parking lot of a strip club that looked like two breasts matched my bewildered heart. *What am I doing? This is crazy. What am I going to say?*

Well, at first I said nothing. I just stood there. Awkward! But I had learned many years ago from one of the wisest men I had ever met—a homeless man in Franklin, Tennessee—that it is the arrogance of Christians that drives us to talk. It is wiser to listen. So I stood for what was probably just a few seconds but felt like eternity. I stood between these two women, one on the right and the other on the left.

They stared me down, eyebrows raised.

I introduced myself. "Hello, I'm Damian Chandler. I'm here preaching revival at such-and-such church."

Cold response.

"How was your day?" I asked them.

Awkwardness to the highest exponent.

Was that a stupid question? I was making a fool of myself.

Their faces each made it plain: *I know what*

this is about and I am not on the clock. The one on my right scooted over, getting as far away from the well-dressed weirdo as she could. The other did not bother to acknowledge my presence. As I talked, she waited, for she had had these types of conversations before and they all had an expected end. A pleasant introduction, quickly cheapened by an invitation to degrade herself. She waited. But the invitation never came.

She was a bruised exterior. Abuse had eaten away at her innocence. The shadows of the strip club were a convenient cover for this wounded woman.

The shadows of shame in which the tree stood, there in my living room, brought this strange place back to my memory, where this woman had sought refuge. Here on the steps, without makeup or outfit, without the cover of shadows, or the whistling of men and the waving money, she sat exposed, naked, like the crooked tree.

Yet, under all the cover-up, her innocence remained, a beauty that was still visible if I looked with God's eyes. I took the time to look at her that way. In the shadows, she was a woman without a name, known for what she did after dark. But here in the light, she was someone's daughter. Quite possibly someone's mother. A human being. A child of God.

I sat down. And sitting on the steps of that strip club, she ignored the stupidity of my questions and somehow she shared her life. Her beginnings. Her hopes. Her dreams. We talked about how she got there. We talked about her getting out one day. A family she had run from, she now wanted to run to. I thought I saw her smile. I invited her to the revival. I knew I would not see her there. Not that night. Probably not ever. But I knew that revival had already happened, and it had happened on the stairs of a strip club.

When the door behind us opened, a UFC fighter came out. A muscle-bound man with a sinister scowl. He stared at me and then nodded at her.

Slowly rising, she grabbed her small bag and asked "Would you pray for me?"

I did pray for her and then I invited her to the revival again.

Then she disappeared behind the door, back to shadows.

She was a crooked Christmas tree. Not because she was a stripper. No! Because she was human.

As I remembered the woman sitting on the steps of that strip club, I was reminded that jacked-up people are loved by God, too. And in God's eyes they are no less jacked up than me. He has a plan for their lives, and though I might give up, turn my face away, walk on the other side, God hopes with stubborn hope I will partner with Him to save what He loves.

My kids never truly saw the tree's condition. They were never scarred by its shameful comparison. They never gave it a degrading name. From the moment they saw it, all they felt was love. And that love resulted in a commitment. And their commitment was greater than its crookedness.

I can't really say that I loved the tree. But the longings for another had faded, and I could now honestly say that I was committed to it.

WHAT-IFS

So we stood, me and my tree. We stood in silence. Silence as awkward as a ninety-year-old woman doing the "Gangnam Style" dance in a miniskirt. It was the kind of silence where you wish you had something to say but you know that anything you could say would be the wrong thing to say. So you say nothing.

That silence took the tree back to an era before the tree had crooked limbs and a deformed trunk. Before its shame. Shame is not a physical attribute. It's not a wayward action. It's not a number on a scale or the fact that you failed. It is the way you feel. It's the way you feel about that physical attribute, the way you feel about that wayward action, the way you feel about that number on the scale or the fact that you failed. It's perception and assumption blended into a toxic concoction.

And the victim of shame is innocence.

Innocence is what I see when my two-year-old jumps the wall of the bathtub like an escapee and refuses to be captured again by the prison called clothes. Nakedness is freedom. He wears his freedom proudly, strutting and dancing across the room without reserve or restraint. He knows that eventual apprehension is his inevitable reality, but this immediate freedom is oh so sweet. So he dodges and dives as long as he can, for he loves to be exposed.

But somewhere between the cradle and the stage, kids learn to love their clothes. Maybe it is the feeling of soft cotton against warm skin. The bite of cold air that attacks as they get out of the water. Maybe it's just too many bedtime readings of Hans Christian Andersen's *The Emperor's New Clothes*. As if a rite of passage, children learn that there is shame in nakedness.

Nakedness with clothes, nakedness with truth, nakedness with God.

Like Adam and Eve, we lose our innocence, pawning freedom for sin's bondage. Sin causes shame, and shame introduces fear, the fear of exposure. So when God comes looking, walking in the cool of the garden, He finds us hiding in the shade of trees far from the Light.* No longer dancing in naked freedom, we now hide in shame, prompting the question, "Who told you that you were naked?"†

We try everything conceivable to cover our shame. Degrees and affluence. Sex and relationships. Work and overwork. All while living in the shadows, trying to disguise our shame. We hide our sin and our guilt as if our fig leaves can camouflage our brokenness.

When we are inevitably exposed, will we run and hide or, forgetting shame, stand—like the crooked tree?

---

* See Genesis 3:8.
† Genesis 3:11

Even as we stand, our knees wobble at the thought of rejection. This is our true fear. The fear that causes us to shrink back. To back away from the Light and hide again in the shadows. Rejection is the fear that rides shotgun with exposure. It whispers loudly. No one else hears the rejection. You hear nothing but rejection. What if they don't like me? What if it doesn't go well? What if I am not as good as I think? What if?

What if I am exposed before God and He rejects me? What if He can't handle my type? What if His love guarantee doesn't cover my kind of brokenness? What if?

These rogue questions leave the mouth, enter ears, and take residence in the heart, quickly morphing into deceptive statements that we find ourselves declaring as truth.

"God will reject me!"

"God can't handle my type!"

"God's love doesn't cover my kind of brokenness!"

There is only one way to dislodge the deception. Until I drop my fig leaves and walk out of the shadows, I never will truly know whether or not God can handle people like me, or if God's love covers, or if I will be rejected. My arms are tired, and my hands are weary. I have held these leaves so long they are now heavy. And so, like the crooked tree, I let them go, and I finally stand before You, out of the shadows, without *shame*. Fully exposed.

COVERED IN MUD

These were deeply thoughtful moments standing there beside my tree. One thought led to another. And I was beamed to a moment in high school in Barbados, at a time when volleyball was the rave. Our school had no gym. No school did. And our gymlessness meant we played outdoors, even during the rainy season, when outdoors meant downpours.

Rain or not, we played our game. But wet conditions were an enemy to me. For I was one part athletic and the other part clumsy. On this day, monsoon conditions joined forces with my clumsiness, creating a typhoon my pride would not withstand. One fatal play. And that clumsiness overthrew my athleticism. It was as if I dove off a diving board into a pool of mud. Mud covered me. My clothes, my shoes, my hair. I washed. I scrubbed. I scraped. But the mud was an alien life-form. And the more I washed, the more it multiplied, refusing to release me. I would have to walk muddy, through town, to catch a bus home...*during rush hour*. All I felt was shame.

The stares of all the passersby let me know that I was the only mud-covered twelve-year-old in Bridgetown, Barbados, that day. I could feel the wind from the whipping necks as my fellow travelers became my judges. Gavel in hand, they stood apart from me. I felt like the leper. A kooky misfit. For my muddiness was unique, unique to me.

Sometimes that unwanted unique feeling returns. And life feels like a long walk down a busy street caked in mud, and muddy alone. I must admit that I've wondered at times if that is God's intention. Was He so hurt by our rejection that He sat back and relished our muddy condition?

But the God I've come to know doesn't want us walking through life with sin's mud caked on our face. There is no staring of His eyes or whipping of His neck. He doesn't want to be right just to prove that I was wrong.* God is not that player who shoots threes with seconds to go, up by thirty. God doesn't throw Hail Marys downfield in a blowout to tattoo shame on our faces, to make us permanently wear a badge of sin.

I have heard enough finger-pointing sermons to feel that way, and to tell the truth I've also preached my fair share. But I know that there is a monumental difference between my mud story and Romans 3:23. The truth is that *all* of humanity is caked in mud and there is nothing clean about us. There is mud everywhere. Under our fingernails and in our hair. And none have been saved from its wicked stains.

Sin's greatest deception is tricking us into

---

* See Romans 3:5–8.

believing that we are alone in our muddiness. But the only one clean is Jesus. He's the only perfectly straight tree.

And Jesus approaches me, not with condemnation and chastisement, but with a towel and some water saying, "Heard you had a spill." He exposes my sin only to clean it up and whispers, "Don't worry. There is no mud my blood can't handle. I got you!"*

As I stood beside the tree, I, for the first time, felt a camaraderie in its crookedness. It was me. I was it. And so I leaned over and whispered to it, "Don't worry, crooked tree. I got you."

* 1 John 1:7.

THE TREE IS IN
THE BUILDING

The tree's unfortunate condition almost blinded me to the most important fact: the tree was in the building! That meant it was time to party. The arrival of the tree was no small matter. We had waited a long time. A very long time—328 days to be exact. On that momentous day, bulbs and lights, long returned to the attic, were going to be brought down again. Finally that day was here!

And so right there beside the crooked tree, I cued happy music and turned it up loud, and we had a party because the tree was in the building. Zoe twirled and danced. Salem did his jig. Levi unsuccessfully did some indescribable movement meant to dislocate his spleen. And I grabbed my wife, and we danced slo-o-ow.

Why? Because the tree was in the building!

Unsuspecting shepherds sat on hills, on what they thought was a normal night. Herd the sheep, count the sheep, fall asleep, then do it again. And again. And again. The only exception to the monotony was the occasional howl of a hungry beast, breaking the night's silence. Night after night on sleepy rolling hills, repetition murdered expectation.

From the bite in Eden to the birth in Bethlehem had been a long time.* A very long time. Long enough to lull sleepy hills to sleep and murder the expectation of waiting humankind.

⤺

But for worlds and planets and soil and sun, this moment would not go unnoticed. They would not allow the endless nights to dull their anticipation for The Day. For stars wrote of

---

* See Genesis 3:6.

His arrival on the pages of the sky, heralding that the long wait was over. Then, as if their celestial display was insufficient, they elected one of their own to announce His location. And at his nomination, that star was so excited that he danced and jigged against the midnight sky, leading men wiser than I, to the place where the baby lay.*

Not just stars but angels. These messengers of light were also a part of the cast. They sat backstage rehearsing notes and lines, full of anxious energy, waiting for the opening night of heaven's greatest play. They were antsy, nervous maybe. The message they would deliver bore such weight that it would shift the world on its axis.

The curtains were drawn and they cued happy music. The sky exploded with sound and light, for they had waited long enough and this night would be the night. And they danced and jigged across the sky singing, shouting,

---

* See Matthew 2:1–12.

"Glory to God in the Highest."* The Tree is in the building.

~

And so, as my family partied around our crooked tree, I could almost hear Jesus saying, "As the angels danced and jigged about me, heaven dances and jigs about you. And Vegas ain't got nothing on that party. You've been lost, and the Father has been waiting for too long. Way too long. Heaven does not wait till you get everything right, till you find a way to straighten your crooked branches. Heaven rejoices because the tree is in the building! And if the tree is in the building, there is no crooked branch that the Father can't fix."

---

* See Luke 2:8–20.

THE ART OF
DECORATING

As the party wound down, it stood there. Still naked, the crooked tree had yet to be covered. But the reason for my pause now had nothing to do with the tree. I knew who the tree was and what the tree needed. But as I looked down at the box of shiny things sitting at my feet, I hated what I saw.

In that moment I had to admit I am a tree snob. I love the Gap. The Gap and Gap Kids. A head-to-toe experience—hat and scarf, sweater and pants, socks and underwear. All colorful. All coordinated. Close my eyes, squint for a bit, and I'm teleported into a box of Skittles. My wacky, warped imagination sees another store in the Gap lineup. Gap Trees! It's that head-to-toe experience, only for the Christmas tree: star and light, bulb and bell, ribbon and skirt, all harmonized like the Blind Boys of Alabama. Coordinated perfection.

But I looked down. And what I saw in my family's box of Christmas ornaments was not Gap Tree perfection. Colorful it was. But most definitely not coordinated.

Nostalgia is an enemy that conspires with my wife against my greatest efforts. It results in irrational reasons for keeping everything: my kid's lost tooth in a Ziploc bag instead of a garbage dump. Rattles and Dora sheets. Onesies that survive twelfth grade. And for the tree? A mishmash of decorations and doodads accumulated over years. A collection as harmonized as a tone-deaf choir. Kindergarten art projects commissioned by sinister teachers who know they would never hang those child-crafted ornaments on their trees, but were resolute on sending them home to mine.

The lack of perfection in that box bothered me. It irritated me. I reached in. Tried to organize. Attempted to arrange. Make some sense of it all. Reds and blues over here. Silver here. Gold here. But the army of color confusion prevailed, and I was left to accept this goulash of imperfect decorations as my fate. How exactly was I to cover imperfection with more imperfection?

I had felt this way before. Actually, I feel this way pretty often. No one has to tell me how flawed I am. I know all too well that I am imperfect. I lie in bed at night meditating on my flaws. My failings, not nightmares, rob me of sleep. My flaws fuel excuse-laden conversations with my wife, my children, my friends, and my congregation. I am always having to say "sorry." Sorry I'm too loud. Sorry I'm too forgetful. Too shallow. Too, too, too. I do not know what it is like to not feel bad about being me. Self is my fatal flaw.

I deal with the fatal flaw of self by covering it with the perfection of decoration. Achievements. Giftings. Talents. All accumulated to distract others from my flawed self. Ornaments to cover my crookedness. I scream at heaven sometimes, and ask why God did not give me a better box of decorations considering all my imperfections.

Then, as I sorted through the decorations in the box, I realized that, pretty or pretty ugly, their purpose was never to cover crookedness. No matter how many shiny things I hung on that tree, it was still going to be crooked. All the Christmas bulbs in the world would never change that fact. They were never meant to.

The answer to my imperfection was no more covering it with my talent than the answer to bad breath is to give that mouth a mic. The gifts that God has placed in my life are meant to give Him pleasure. He has given me a way to make Him happy. Shiny things that glow for Him, and not for me. Gifts to glorify the Giver, not to cover the crooked. The decorations are not about the tree at all!

So I sat back. I watched my wife smile as she nostalgically enjoyed unwinding each string of old-fashioned colored bulbs. I listened to my kids squeal with glee to see each of their class projects unwrapped from last year's newspaper. I imagined the joy I would feel in watching them glory in it all, when the decorations were finally hoisted in place. That uncoordinated, discombobulated assortment of random shiny things became beautiful in my sight. The imperfect box was perfect.

"MOM, IT'S GARBAGE!"

Did I mention that the reason that the decorations in the Christmas box got so discombobulated in the first place is because of my wife's tendency to listen to nostalgia's lying tongue? Like a snake, nostalgia hisses at her, "Has your husband truly said that thou shalt not save another thing?" And so, a tissue one of our kids sneezed in at birth ends up hung on our Christmas tree reincarnated as a snowflake. She simply does not see garbage as garbage.

And neither does my mother. (They say guys marry their mothers. Whoever "they" is needs to keep their nose outta my business.)

My mother and wife are two uniquely beautiful and wonderful women. But...there are a lot of similarities, beginning with their inability to see garbage as garbage.

Mom saves everything. In her eyes there is no such thing as garbage because everything can be repurposed. Whenever Mom visits, she stores the meal we had two weeks ago, washes freezer bags for reuse, smuggles plastic bottles back to her church for some crazy VBS art project. Maybe it is because she grew up poor in a small village in Barbados where they could not afford to throw things away, and often other people's garbage became their treasure. But even when money was no longer a problem, the drive to salvage never went away.

But it is not just an urge to salvage but to transform. The chicken from the night before becomes a stew, and the three-day-old rice passes the sniff inspection and goes into the frying pan with butter. Her creations even garnered names: "Cookup," "Stew food." Mom just opened a pot and threw in every leftover with a dash of prayer. And when she was done, the leftovers were even better than the original meal.

What my mother could do with so little fascinated me. She seemed to relish the challenge of not just making do, but making it the best. Hand on hip, she scratched her head and said, "Okay. Leave it to me." The older I get, the more I love to hear those words because I know that what is coming next is going to wow me. Mom has the gift of transformation.

And not just with food. But also with people. There was always some kid who called her "mum" but never came down her birth canal. The children people ignored. The ones people expected little of. Those were the ones who seemed to be her favorites. She could see what they could be and was willing to make the love investment needed to see the desired transformation. Sometimes the end result was tragic. Love rejected, kindness taken advantage of. But her bandaged wounds never stopped her from opening her arms. "Okay. Leave 'em to me."

Mom is one of God's transformation agents. She is called to a ministry of repurposing. Her eyes see the beauty and her heart already sees their new end. A new conclusion to their story. To walk away from them would be to walk away from herself. God gave my mother His eyes and His heart. To see the world as He sees it. Not for what it is but for what it could be.

The universe moans in frustration*: "God, how long are you going to extend yourself to those human knuckleheads? Those ungrateful wretches? How long, God, shall mercy make a mockery of grace?" I can see Him now, hand on hip. "Okay, leave them to me."

God says, "Look in my fridge. Look in my cupboards. There is nothing but brokenness and chaos. They are the only ingredients I have left." God is busy cooking up something special with us, living leftovers. Thank God for

---

* See Romans 8:22.

the ministry of transformation. And not just transformation but repurposing.

I looked at the tree now and realized that something was missing. "Hand me that snotty-tissue snowflake ornament thingy." I hung it, now not with a wall view, but in full view.

GIVE ME SOME BOOYAH

My kids ran toward the crooked tree, happy, unable to appreciate all that it (and I) had been through.

"Is it time now, Dad? Can we decorate it now?"

"Yup!"

"Finally!"

They jumped at that tree like linebackers on a fumble. Tore open the boxes that held the decorations.

I closed my eyes and told myself, *They are having fun. Leave it alone.* For the most part, I ignored the lack of symmetry. Lights, Christmas bulbs, art pieces they made, snowflakes and snowmen, all disproportionately hung at the limits of their heights. Nothing hung above the four-foot bar set by my older daughter's reach, and a flood of bling circled the two-foot valley that my youngest son lived in.

Far beyond the reach of their hands, a lonely branch sat atop the crooked tree, awaiting its reward. Every Christmas tree wished for, longed for, that moment when its highest branch would proudly bear the weight of the star. Sitting near the window, our tree could see across the street, where every other tree had already received this brilliant crowning. It wondered if its moment would ever come. Because every tree, even a crooked one, wanted some BOOYAH.

The late, great Stuart Scott in his color commentary on *SportsCenter*, at the end of some crushing homerun, ridiculous catch, incredible dunk, would fill his lungs slowly with the necessary air and, in concert with every man and sport-loving woman across the nation, shout in chorus, at the top of his lungs, "BOOYAH!"

"Booyah" is for any moment where confetti should fall from the ceiling or fireworks explode across the sky. It is a celebration. Not just of sports. But of all things good. That crowning moment. The festivity of your child's first independent visit to the toilet. The glee of finally getting that first minimum-wage paycheck. The excitement of realizing that the test you failed is the one the teacher dropped. It is pure joy, where the only appropriate response is to stretch your hands wide and shout at the tip-top of your lungs, "BOOYAH!"

It was only right to give the tree some Booyah. For all it had fought through, to simply be standing deserved a celebration. And so I would begrudge it no longer. It was finally going to get what it had waited to receive. A star atop its loftiest branch.

Now, if it had seen the star that I pulled out of the box, it might not have been as excited. Some stars twinkle. They dazzle eyes with dancing lights. They sit on treetop, perching and shouting "Look at my glory!" Unfortunately, that is not our star. It is the oldest decoration we have. It never had the dancing lights. And never once in its life did it shout "Booyah!" It's just not that kind of star. It is string and metal held together like a first-grade art project. The stingily sprinkled glitter it once bore long since died. Sorry star it is. But a star it still is.

~

It's not really the star that makes the Booyah. It's the moment. The *moment* we waited for. The *moment* we faced and fought for and won is the true reward.

I wonder about heaven sometimes. John tells us about a lot of dazzling and dancing things. Streets of gold, gates of pearl, mansions and seas. All far beyond what my imagination can see. But none of that makes heaven for me. What makes me want to be there is the moment my Savior walks in my direction, smile on face, crown in nail-pierced hands, and He places that crown on my head and says, "Well *done."** And I don't care what kind of crown it is. The purest gold covered in carats of diamonds or cheap plastic made in a factory in China. It won't matter to me. For it was never the material of the reward. The real reward for me was always the moment. That *moment* is what I await. It's what I fight for. It's what Jesus fought for, for me. And it will be worth the wait.

So if my translation to heaven does not result in earthly amnesia, and you want to know where in heaven I am, just listen for the echoing sound. Because I'm gonna fill my lungs with heaven's rarified air, tilt my holy head back, and scream at the top of my sanctified lungs, "BOOYAH!" And when you hear it, you will know that either Stuart made it or that is Damian Chandler.

I approached the tree with this sorry star. It showed no signs of disdain. It did not raise its eyebrows or turn away its trunk in disgust. As

---

* See Matthew 25:21.

I climbed the step ladder, it seemed to lower its lofty branch. And then in pride, my crooked tree straightened its deformed spine and bore that star, its reward. And I think I heard it say, "Booyah!"

DO IT YOURSELF

The tree was decorated. Kinda. Putting all those ornaments on was like putting twenties on a hoopty that doesn't even start, because the tree was *still leaning*. I caught the vision that there must be a solution to the crookedness of my tree. Although the kids were oblivious to its plight, its issues were obvious to me. Obvious problems often come packaged with obscure answers.

Back in the garage, I looked around and said to myself, *Man, I got a lot of books.* Book collecting is every pastor's hobby and secret addiction, right? Late at night we steal away to forbidden lands and smuggle books into our houses, undetected by policing spouses. We need our books. We place dog-eared decoys on our desks so the naive think we actually read them, and we use the rest to keep lonely boxes company, and empty garages full.

Sitting next to one of those boxes was a home-repair, do-it-yourself book that I promise you I had all intentions of reading. It was one of those books you buy before you start the project you will never finish. I grabbed that book and finally realized its purpose. I shoved it under one of the legs of the tree stand, figuring that it would correct the lean. Disaster! The tree looked more crooked than it did before.

I mused about this. Salvation is not a do-it-yourself project. You would think that since we humans mess up, we would be best equipped to make it right. Since no one knows me like me, it stands to reason that there is no one better to fix me than me. I hear it all the time: "I'll come back to church when I fix this." "I can't pray again until I stop doing this or that."

Do It Yourself is the slogan of modern Christianity: Seven steps to this, ten steps to that. A chapter a day. The Bible in a year. None of these are bad necessarily, but we can, without realizing it, use them as do-it-yourself props we lean on to avoid seeking out the Handyman, the expert, God.

If I could change myself, I would have. If I could fix this hopeless mess, it would have been fixed. But I can't. No one can. And I don't need to. God took on my life as His "Do It Himself" project. He became a man and subbed into the game to fix what the first man, Adam, had broken.* Clutch move. Clutch God.

So the do-it-yourself book didn't work, but I had not yet given up on the book idea, and grabbed a few paperbacks, all Christian books, small devotionals I had collected at conferences and never intended to read. I placed several of them under each leg of the tree. Unlike the DIY encyclopedia, these books were small and the change they made was incremental. But each book was significant enough to give the leg it supported exactly what it needed.

---

* See 1 Corinthians 15:45–49 and Romans 5:12–21.

It was hard to see how a tree with problems that big could be fixed with adjustments that seemed so small.

That was exactly my thought when I first went to a physical therapist. My back was so hurt I was sure it was broken. I wanted that therapist to bend me up like a pretzel and crack my spine in half. Instead? Breathe in. Breathe out. Relax. Ice and then heat. Stretch this. Flex that. Sometimes the movements were so small I would think to myself this could not possibly be doing anything. These people were just taking my money.

Then I married a physical therapist in training. I became a willing test monkey. I learned that the physical therapists' answer to every ailment is ice. And when that doesn't work, try heat. Here she comes with yet another manipulation.

"Feel that?"

"No!"

"How about that?"

"Negative! What I feel is that this school

is sucking up all our money and robbing us blind."

But then it happened. Little by little, I did start to feel it. Small changes here. Fewer aches there. I was beginning to see that sometimes it is the small adjustments that correct the largest issues.

Our problem isn't small, and it is not imagined. Sin. The true cause of my crookedness. Sin is a large, complicated mess. It stands to reason that the remedy would need to be just as complex. But no, Jesus simply came. Not from the big city or some swanky burb but from the side of town that never produced anything worth producing.* And He did not look the part. Not draped in a Ralph Lauren jacket and Dolce & Gabbana slacks. No Armani watch to declare that this was the most epic time in Earth's history. No. Isaiah 53:2 says that there was nothing sexy about His appearance. He was simple. And many could not accept

---

* See John 1:46.

Him as the long-awaited answer to such a complex problem. And so the only people at His inaugural press conference were some strange-looking foreigners and a few shepherds still covered in their stink. The solution seemed to be too simple to fit the problem.

When we find ourselves facing the complicated mess, the monstrous wall, impossible odds, we anticipate an answer whose magnitude matches the madness. For that seems to us to be the appropriate response, but not to God. Jesus-sized answers are often big blessings in small boxes. God's answer to our complicated sin problem is too simple for us to accept. And so we ignore His simple brilliance and keep looking for the *real* answer.

The tree was crooked. It had a mean lean. But the answer was not the big do-it-yourself encyclopedia but small and simple books. After I placed them carefully under each leg, the corner in which the tree stood agreed to be the keeper of its secrets, and I surrendered the remaining blemishes to its care. I gently placed the tree skirt over the whole engineered mess, not desiring it to be exposed. And then I stepped back to take a look.

Once my angst had raged against it. I had looked at it with folded fist and clenched jaw. But now it was beauty. It was beauty not born of copy or pattern, but an unexpected beauty unique and wonderful. It was a beauty that was not so much created by me, as much as I was allowed to perceive it. And that, my friends, is the most beautiful beauty there is.

The Crooked Tree would no longer be remembered by that name. It no longer fit. This was now the Beautiful Tree. And that change happened one small book at a time.

LIGHTED MESS

The whole process was way too long. Before the last bulb was hung, my kids had been long gone. As I stood there, I couldn't help but think, *What a lighted mess!*

Didn't spend too much time looking at the tree. There was too much cleaning up to do, three kids to bathe and put to bed. But late that night, when the house was silent of running feet and shrieking screams, no music blasting, no question asking, I finally stood still and took it all in. In the darkness, its light was the only light. Pinks and blues and greens reflecting off glass ornaments. So beautiful. No sign, no remembrance of troubled beginnings, it now begged to be showered with gifts.

And breaking my silence, speaking through

the dark, God said, "Beautiful, isn't it? But suppose this tree boasted of its beauty and its straightness, never for a second giving credit to the books beneath its skirt. How crazy would that be?" Then God bent down, got to the ear level of His son so as to whisper. "Don't you ever forget that you are nothing more than a crooked tree, propped up by grace."

I bowed my head, and I cried.

A lighted mess is what I am. He chose me, redeemed me, and left no evidence of my troubled beginnings. By grace He propped me up and then did something crazy. He put His light on a crooked tree and said, "Now you go light up the world."

ON THE CURB

Christmas doesn't last forever and I am glad. The first time I hear "Jingle Bells" I feel like dancing. The last time I hear "Jingle Bells" I feel like barfing. No more red and green. My temporary blindness is healed the day after Christmas and I finally realize that red and green don't go together. Santa ain't real. Frosty has melted. I feel like getting a big box to imprison every shiny Christmas bulb, every string of multicolored lights. A scrooge I am not, but a scrooge I become the day after Christmas.

Wrapping paper and boxes purchased with excitement and care sit in recycling bins awaiting an uncertain fate. Long lines of the Anxious who awaited their turn to swipe their card and grab a bag are now longer lines of the Angry waiting to return what they once waited to buy. None of this makes sense.

Another thing my post-Christmas eyesight reveals is that live Christmas trees are a big mess. Pine needles are everywhere. On the floor. On the stairs. On the couch. In my wife's hair. And you can't get rid of them. They are like pop-ups on a PC. Every time you remove one, up pops another. After the gifts are gone and the smell has faded, I am left with one big headache.

Oh, the folly of it all. The tree we dressed, we eventually undress. We take our lights back and drag that tree out the same door we brought it in. Then we take the box of ornaments and the stand that held that crooked tree, and return them all to their exile. The darkest and the farthest corner of the garage.

Funny how we spend our days building up, only to tear down. And so all was where all started. A crooked tree dressed, then undressed, awaiting the fate reserved for things whose season has passed.

We had counted the days till we bought the tree. Now we counted the days till we could get rid of it. What good was a Christmas tree after we had pillaged all of its gifts? After emerald shine shone no more, and dingy brown replaced glorious green. The tree was now as useful as sunscreen in Seattle, and as yesterday as a boom box with high-speed dubbing (depending on your age you might have to look that one up). Its days were over and it had to go. It occupied space in my house but paid no rent.

But I could not serve its eviction notice until I had the date. The garbage company sent notice of the date when all trees would meet their fate, and every house awaited that day to deliver their tree to the gallows.

When that day finally came, down the street, down the driveway, every neighbor dragged their tree by its ankles to its end. Every family, including the *other* family, the one from the store. Yes, even the tree of trees, the one that spun on pointed toes, hoisted above their heads like a tree hero. That tree met my *crooked tree* again, and despite its fame, their end was the same. They both were dumped on the curb.

A new year starts and we move on from our revelry into the next season, forgetting the short-lived joy of what was just past. Maybe this was the confusion of Solomon. The wise man was made foolish by the irony of life, that no matter your start, your rise, your shine, the end of every tree is exactly the same. No matter the season, its beauty, its success, every season, every generation will end like the rest.* They all end up dumped on the curb.

But there is beauty in these ashes. Because though my tree must have known its fate, it never once refused to shine or dance. In fact, the brevity of its moment probably made it feel the urgency to live its short life purposefully. And so the brief life of my tree was better than the longer life of others.

---

* See Ecclesiastes 1:1–11.

MAYBE

So I dragged the crooked tree out the door and sat it on the same driveway that had first received it. And then, outside my house, I bore the saw. Limbs now limp, the tree understood how this was going to go. There was no cry for a change of my mind. No attempt to remind me of how much joy it had brought to the season. Was there no arguable defense? No attorney to speak on its behalf? Would it enter a guilty plea without calling on even one witness?

As if taught by those that went before, it understood that this was its lot. The brown tinge of tired leaves gave indication that its time had come. And so it lifted broken branches, willingly exposing trunk to chain saw's teeth.

And...on that driveway, the tree bled its dust and died.

I dragged the tree, cut in three pieces, to the curb, callously throwing it into the street. Later that day, the garbage truck hauled it away, leaving a remnant of pine needles where it had lain. And thus ends the story of my *crooked tree*.

Maybe.

The tree was eventually shredded, its chips turned into compost. And that compost added to soil, brought life to something new that grew in that soil.

Those who once hailed him joined cynical crowds of scoffers who together raised their voices, crying, "Crucify him! Crucify him!"* And crucify Him they did. They dragged Him

---

* Luke 23:21

out of Pilate's palace. They believed they had a right to. For had they not made Him who He was? Didn't His fame ride on their praises?

"We built you up. We will tear you down."

Think about everything Jesus could have said.

You made Me? I made everything. In the beginning was Me. I was God and I was with God.*

With one word He could have snatched their breath, commanded their heart to cease its beating and their blood to cease flowing. With one word He could have commanded the skies to fold up and the sun to retreat. But there was no request for deliverance or attempt to escape.

They dragged Him out the city gates. Possibly down the same streets where people with palm branches hailed Him as King.† Now scoffs and spitting replaced their praises. But He said

---

* See John 1:1.
† See Matthew 21:9.

nothing.* No reminder to His executioners of healings or feedings. Surely there was someone in the crowd who had lost leprous† spots or eaten the blessed loaves.‡ If there was, they would hear no appeal from Him. Not a word of defense. He understood His purpose and "...like a lamb to the slaughter" He was silent, "...he did not open his mouth."§

And they killed Him. They mercilessly murdered Jesus.

They killed the tree, chopping it down. Dancing on its stump as though they already had the trophy. Their arrogance was fueled by their confidence in its demise. But they underestimated the power of the tree, and its seed. It had said, "And do not fear those who kill the body but cannot kill the soul."¶ And though it was true that its trunk was fallen, its roots were yet strong.

---

* See Mark 15:3–5.
† See John 20:1–10.
‡ See Matthew 14:13–21.
§ Isaiah 53:7
¶ Matthew 10:28

And so in the shadow of death's darkness, there was light, and that stump grew branches. And from those branches, leaves. And then fruit. And in three days the stump that they danced on was the tree they bowed to.*

Jesus shook death free, folded his burial clothes, and walked out of that tomb in victory.† Somewhere in the dark of that tomb the tree deposited seed. And the power of resurrection that was His became ours. To every stump Jesus declares the words "and if the spirit of him who raised [Me] from the dead is living in you," you, too, will grow your branches again, "because of his spirit who lives in you."‡

This is as much my story as it is yours. You might not have known it before today, but God has been busy writing His story into yours. His beauty on your crookedness. And that crookedness is a necessary part of the narrative. For

---

* See Luke 24:1–12.
† See John 20:1–10.
‡ Romans 8:11

the beauty of stars is best seen on the darkest nights. The view of mountains more majestic from the deep crevasses of valleys. So don't try to cover it up. Let God's grace do the covering and then you use your life's story to fertilize the roots of another crooked tree.

ABOUT THE AUTHOR

Damian Chandler was born in Toronto, Canada, and raised on the island of Barbados. His ministry journey started in a small church housed in the basement of his home. With only nine members, the burden of the ministry fell equally on the shoulders of all, including sixteen-year-old Damian. At night he could hear the prayers of these humble people rising through the vents into his room. That small church created his spiritual hunger and formed the foundation of his call to ministry.

He holds a masters in Divinity; founded Impact Youth Ministries, an urban youth ministry focused on developing teens with a contagious and fearless faith, and has served churches in Seattle, Huntsville, and now Sacramento, where he is senior pastor of Capitol City Seventh-day Adventist Church.

Damian is passionate about ministry but he is even more passionate about family. After years of dedicated pursuit, God gave him the desire of his heart and a partner in life, his wife, Tanzy Chandler. They later added to their partnership daughter Zoe and sons Salem and Levi.